TOWNSVILLE
AND MAGNETIC ISLAND

PETER LIK

P E T E R   L I K

"My total dedication and obsession with
photography has taken me on journeys
into many remarkable areas throughout
Australia.
I captured this collection of images
using a specialist panoramic camera.
Because of the wider field of view, this
format enables me to portray the true
spirit of Australia on film. Upon viewing
these images I am sure you will share
with me the tranquillity and solitude
I experienced whilst exploring the
stunning beauty of this country."

peter lik PUBLISHING

PO Box 2529 Cairns Queensland 4870 Australia
Telephone: (07) 4053 9000 **Fax:** (07) 4032 1277
sales@peterlik.com.au   **www.peterlik.com**

© **Peter Lik Publishing**   BK15

ISBN **1 876 58501 3**

Front cover - Castle Hill overlooks Townsville and Harbour
Back cover - Early morning colours illuminate Alma Bay
                     on Magnetic Island

Additional Photography - Paul Hamilton

Townsville, Australia's largest tropical city, is surrounded by the grandeur of the Great Barrier Reef, spectacular World Heritage Rainforests and the colourful outback. The city is a charming blend of old and new, rich in history and culture. The tropical city has a culturally diverse population of 130,000 and is renowned for its climate, boasting more than 300 sunny days each year.

Castle Hill (268m high) offers magnificent views of the city, Magnetic Island, rich sugarlands and the Palm group of islands.

Many historic and handsome buildings present themselves, particularly in the waterfront park area, The Strand, and Flinders Street.

The city and region offer a diversity of experiences, that vary from the worlds largest living reef Aquarium, Omnimax Theatre, the excitement of a vibrant nightlife, to a world class casino. Nearby Magnetic Island, listed as a National Park, boasts over 20 palm-fringed bays, superb swimming, snorkelling and hiking.

Further north lie exotic islands such as Orpheus, Hinchinbrook, Dunk and Bedarra, each with their own unique beaches and tropical landscapes.

The Great Barrier Reef is easily accessible from Townsville by luxury catamaran. The pristine azure waters of Kelso Reef offer magnificent snorkelling and diving whilst exploring one of the seven natural wonders of the world.

Inland and west of Townsville, the ghost-like town of Ravenswood retains its historic charm from the gold mining days. Charters Towers boasts classic Victorian, Edwardian and colonial architecture. Further west, fascinating Undara Lava tubes are a must to be explored.

Coconut palms silhouetted by a tropical sunrise at Rowes Bay.

$\mathcal{T}$ownsville's magnificent climate boasts over 300 dry sunny tropical days per year. Located near the same parallel as the Fiji Islands and 1500kms north of the state capital, Brisbane, it is one of the closest Australian cities to the Pacific. Tropical, tranquil bays and exotic islands are situated nearby in the surrounding Coral Sea and offer superb diving and swimming.

Previous page: Castle Hill overlooks Townsville and Harbour

Quaint gazebo on The Strand.

Townsville has a rich history and surprising cultural depth. The cities heritage has been retained in the form of well-preserved civic, commercial and domestic buildings dating back to the regions European settlement in the late 19th century. In addition the city is complemented by nearby significant Aboriginal tribal areas that feature cave art and paintings.

A classic "Queenslander" house nestled beneath Castle Hill.

Daybreak casts its glow over Cleveland Bay with Castle Hill in the background.

Sunset pier, The Strand.

A 180° panoramic vista of Townsville with Magnetic Island in the background

Townsville's port provides an idyllic anchorage.

Aerial view of The Strand.

A tropical beach scene - Hinchinbrook Island.

Aerial view of magnificent Hinchinbrook Island.

Hinchinbrook is the largest whole-island National Park in the world.

Crystal Creek cascades beneath this historic stone bridge at Paluma.

The sheer 305m drop of Wallaman Falls it the longest permanent clear drop waterfall in Australia.

Blencoe Falls.

Paluma.

Wallaman Falls in the wet season.

Undara Dawn

Charters Towers retains its charm from the gold mining days.

The grand architecture of the Imperial Hotel in the ghost-like town of Ravenswood, west of Townsville.

A catamaran glides across turquoise waters at Kelso Reef.

Previous page: Orpheus Island.

Exploring the Great Barrier Reef off Townsville.

Clownfish take refuge in their colourful anemone.

The vibrant colours of fish and coral on the Great Barrier Reef.

MAGNETIC ISLAND

One of the suburbs of Townsville is Magnetic Island, just eight kms or 30 minutes by regular, fast ferry from the city centre.

More than 2000 people live on the island, but nearly three-quarters of its 5.184 hectares is national park. This is criss-crossed by about 20 kilometres of walking tracks winding through pockets of rainforest and stands of eucalyptus, through lush gullies and to the peaks of granite hills that offer delightful views to the many islands of the Coral Sea.

There are more than 20 bays and palm-fringed beaches surruounding the island. Some are accessible by road, with the more secluded being reached via bush tracks or from the sea.

One of the delights of Magnetic Island is the variety of native wildlife. It's known as the "Koala Capital of Australia" with literally thousands of koalas living in the wild. There are also big populations of possums, rock wallabies, curlews, hawks, eagles and parrots. In fact, ardent birdwathcers say it is possible to spot about 160 species of Magnetic Island birdlife.

Buses run regularly between the island settlements, while visitors who wish to be more independent can hire bicycles, mopeds, mini mokes and other vehicles.

The turquoise waters of Arthur Bay.

Previous page: Coconut palms fringe the shores of Horseshoe Bay, Magnetic Island.

Relaxing at Balding Bay.

Fishing beneath a peaceful sunset, Magnetic Island.

Fiery skies, Magnetic Island.

Dramatic landscape at Arthurs Bay.

Previous page: The tranquil waters of Alma Bay, Magnetic Island.

The mini moke provides the ultimate tropical transport on the island.

Horseshoe Bay.

Alma Bay.

Magnetic Island is known as the koala capital of Australia.

*O*ne of the attractions of Magnetic Island is the variety of native wildlife. Thousands of koalas live in the wild and there are large populations of rock wallabies, curlews, hawks, eagles and parrots. Ardent birdwatchers say it's possible to spot about 160 species of birdlife on Magnetic Island.

Daybreak over sculptured sands, West Point, Magnetic Island.

Low tide leaves streaked patterns etched in the sand, Alma Bay.

Arthur Bay boasts a perfect beach.

The picturesque cove of Florence Bay.

BOOKS BY PETER LIK

- Australia
- Blue Mountains
- Brisbane
- Byron Bay
- Cairns
- Daintree and Cape Tribulation
- Fraser Island
- Gold Coast
- Great Barrier Reef
- Port Douglas
- Sunshine Coast
- Sydney
- The Red Centre
- Townsville and Magnetic Island
- Whitsundays
- Wildlife
- World Heritage Rainforest

LARGE FORMAT PUBLICATIONS

- Australia - Images of a Timeless Land
- San Francisco
- Spirit of America

peter lik PUBLISHING